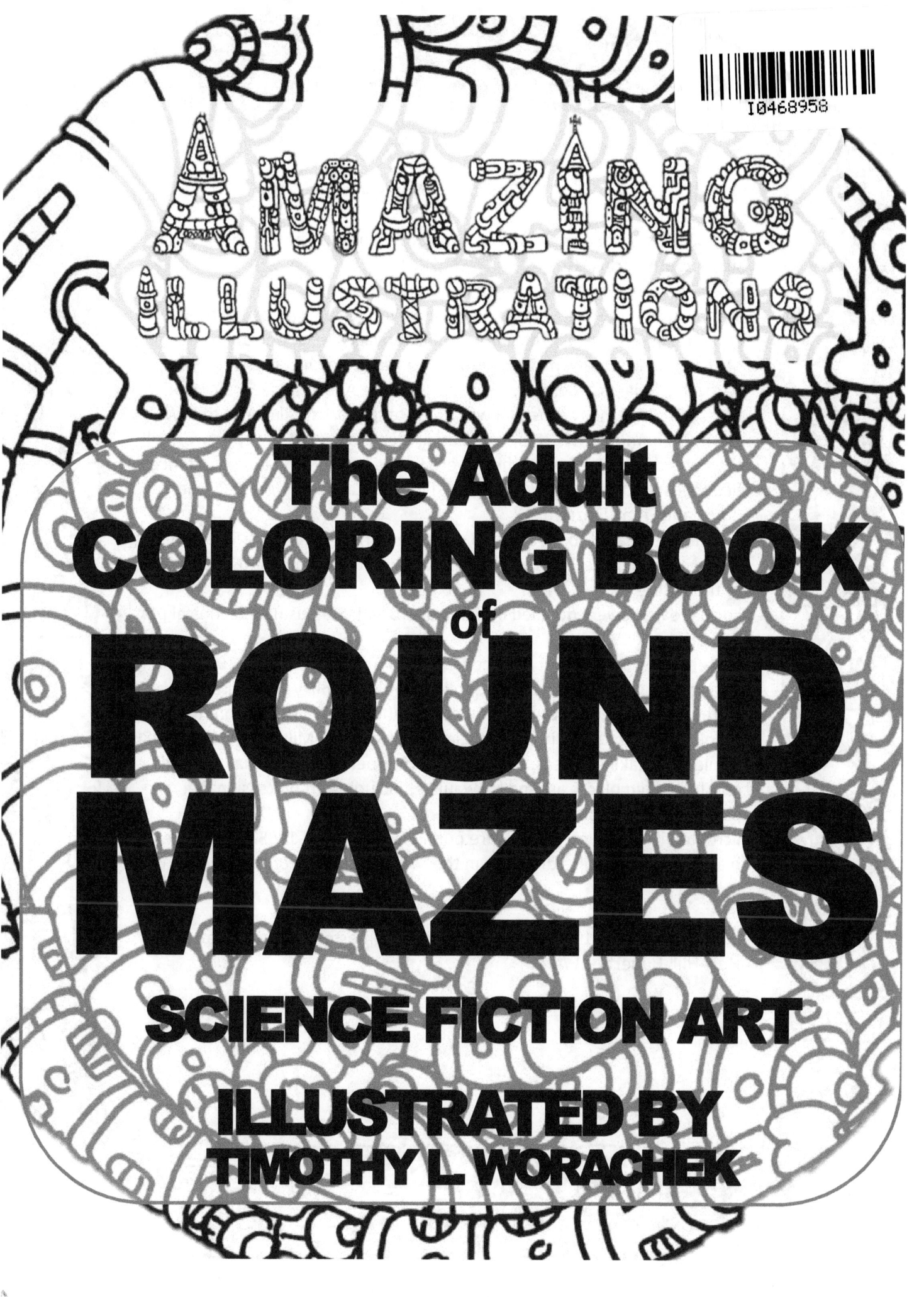

AMAZING
ILLUSTRATIONS

The Adult
COLORING BOOK
of
ROUND
MAZES

SCIENCE FICTION ART

ILLUSTRATED BY
TIMOTHY L WORACHEK

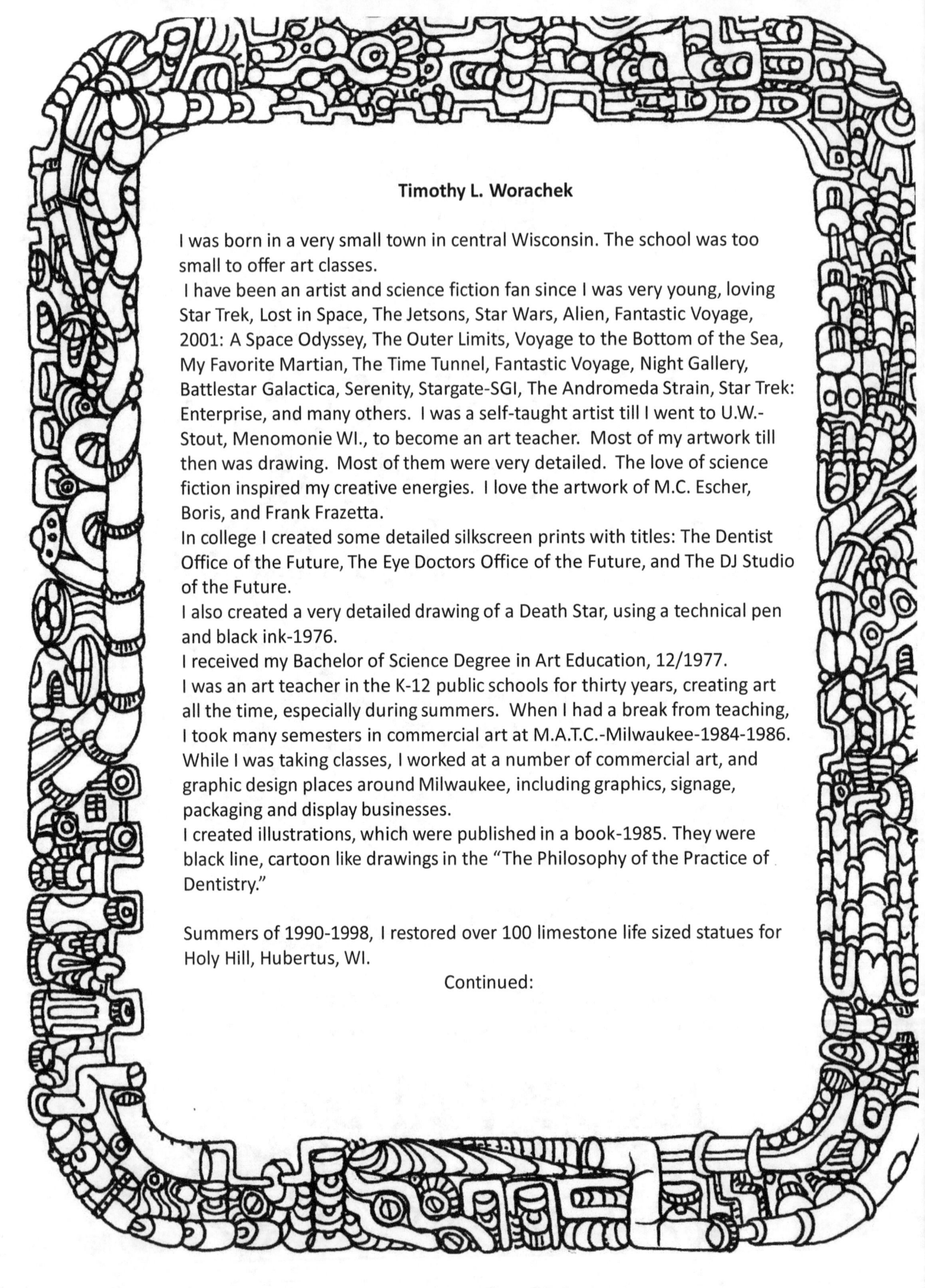

Timothy L. Worachek

I was born in a very small town in central Wisconsin. The school was too small to offer art classes.

I have been an artist and science fiction fan since I was very young, loving Star Trek, Lost in Space, The Jetsons, Star Wars, Alien, Fantastic Voyage, 2001: A Space Odyssey, The Outer Limits, Voyage to the Bottom of the Sea, My Favorite Martian, The Time Tunnel, Fantastic Voyage, Night Gallery, Battlestar Galactica, Serenity, Stargate-SGI, The Andromeda Strain, Star Trek: Enterprise, and many others. I was a self-taught artist till I went to U.W.-Stout, Menomonie WI., to become an art teacher. Most of my artwork till then was drawing. Most of them were very detailed. The love of science fiction inspired my creative energies. I love the artwork of M.C. Escher, Boris, and Frank Frazetta.

In college I created some detailed silkscreen prints with titles: The Dentist Office of the Future, The Eye Doctors Office of the Future, and The DJ Studio of the Future.

I also created a very detailed drawing of a Death Star, using a technical pen and black ink-1976.

I received my Bachelor of Science Degree in Art Education, 12/1977.

I was an art teacher in the K-12 public schools for thirty years, creating art all the time, especially during summers. When I had a break from teaching, I took many semesters in commercial art at M.A.T.C.-Milwaukee-1984-1986. While I was taking classes, I worked at a number of commercial art, and graphic design places around Milwaukee, including graphics, signage, packaging and display businesses.

I created illustrations, which were published in a book-1985. They were black line, cartoon like drawings in the "The Philosophy of the Practice of Dentistry."

Summers of 1990-1998, I restored over 100 limestone life sized statues for Holy Hill, Hubertus, WI.

Continued:

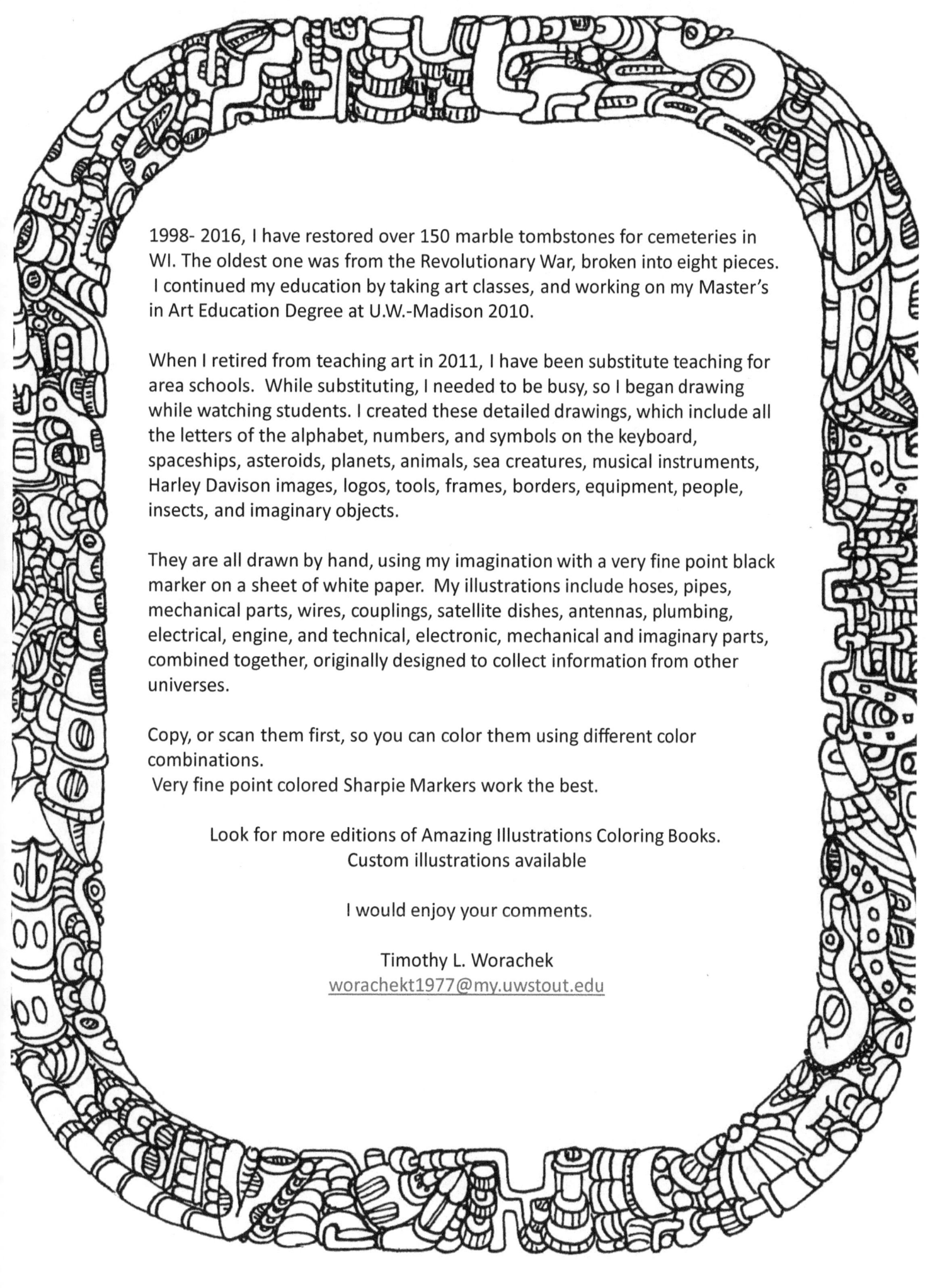

1998- 2016, I have restored over 150 marble tombstones for cemeteries in WI. The oldest one was from the Revolutionary War, broken into eight pieces. I continued my education by taking art classes, and working on my Master's in Art Education Degree at U.W.-Madison 2010.

When I retired from teaching art in 2011, I have been substitute teaching for area schools. While substituting, I needed to be busy, so I began drawing while watching students. I created these detailed drawings, which include all the letters of the alphabet, numbers, and symbols on the keyboard, spaceships, asteroids, planets, animals, sea creatures, musical instruments, Harley Davison images, logos, tools, frames, borders, equipment, people, insects, and imaginary objects.

They are all drawn by hand, using my imagination with a very fine point black marker on a sheet of white paper. My illustrations include hoses, pipes, mechanical parts, wires, couplings, satellite dishes, antennas, plumbing, electrical, engine, and technical, electronic, mechanical and imaginary parts, combined together, originally designed to collect information from other universes.

Copy, or scan them first, so you can color them using different color combinations.
Very fine point colored Sharpie Markers work the best.

Look for more editions of Amazing Illustrations Coloring Books.
Custom illustrations available

I would enjoy your comments.

Timothy L. Worachek
worachekt1977@my.uwstout.edu

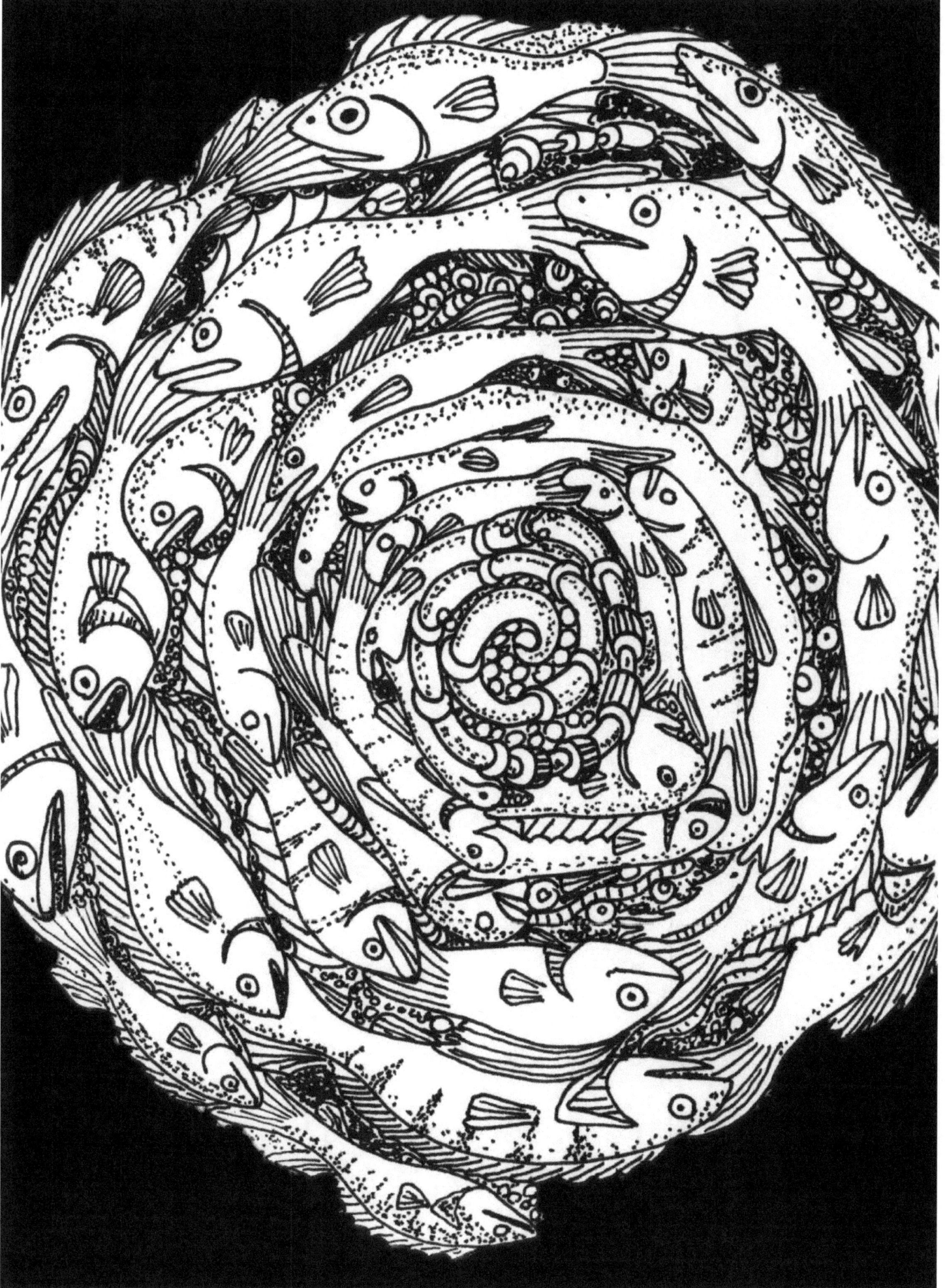

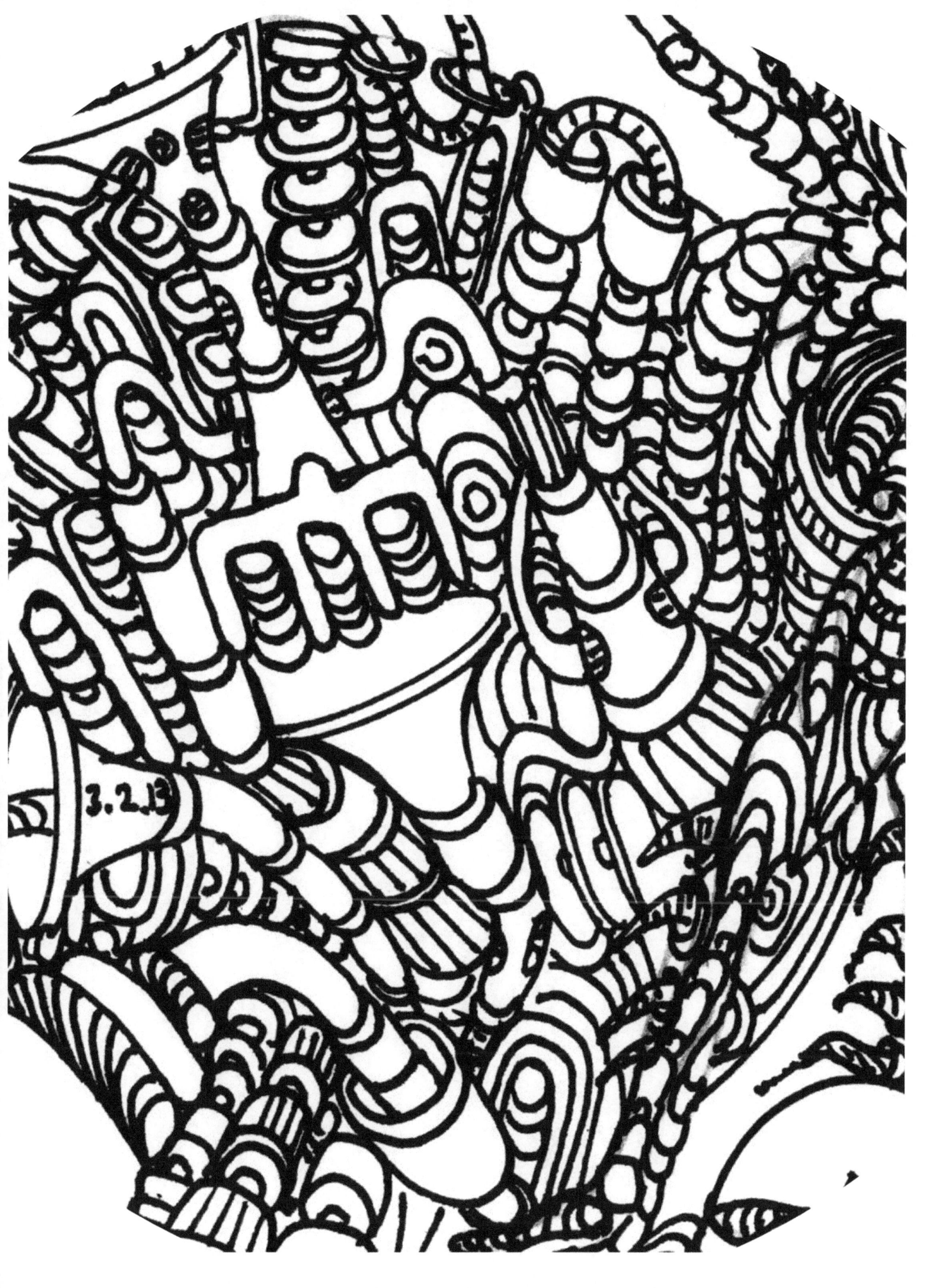

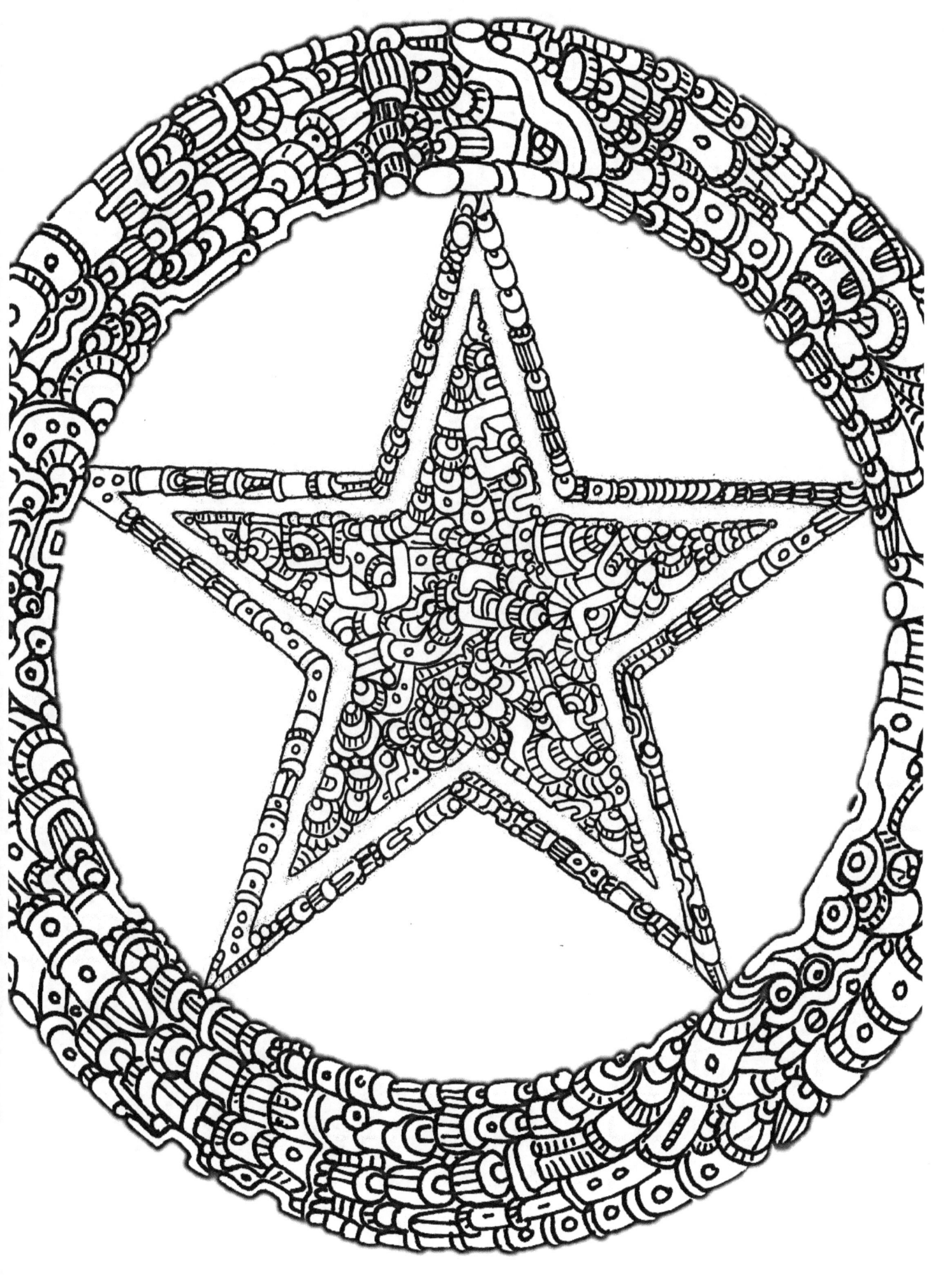

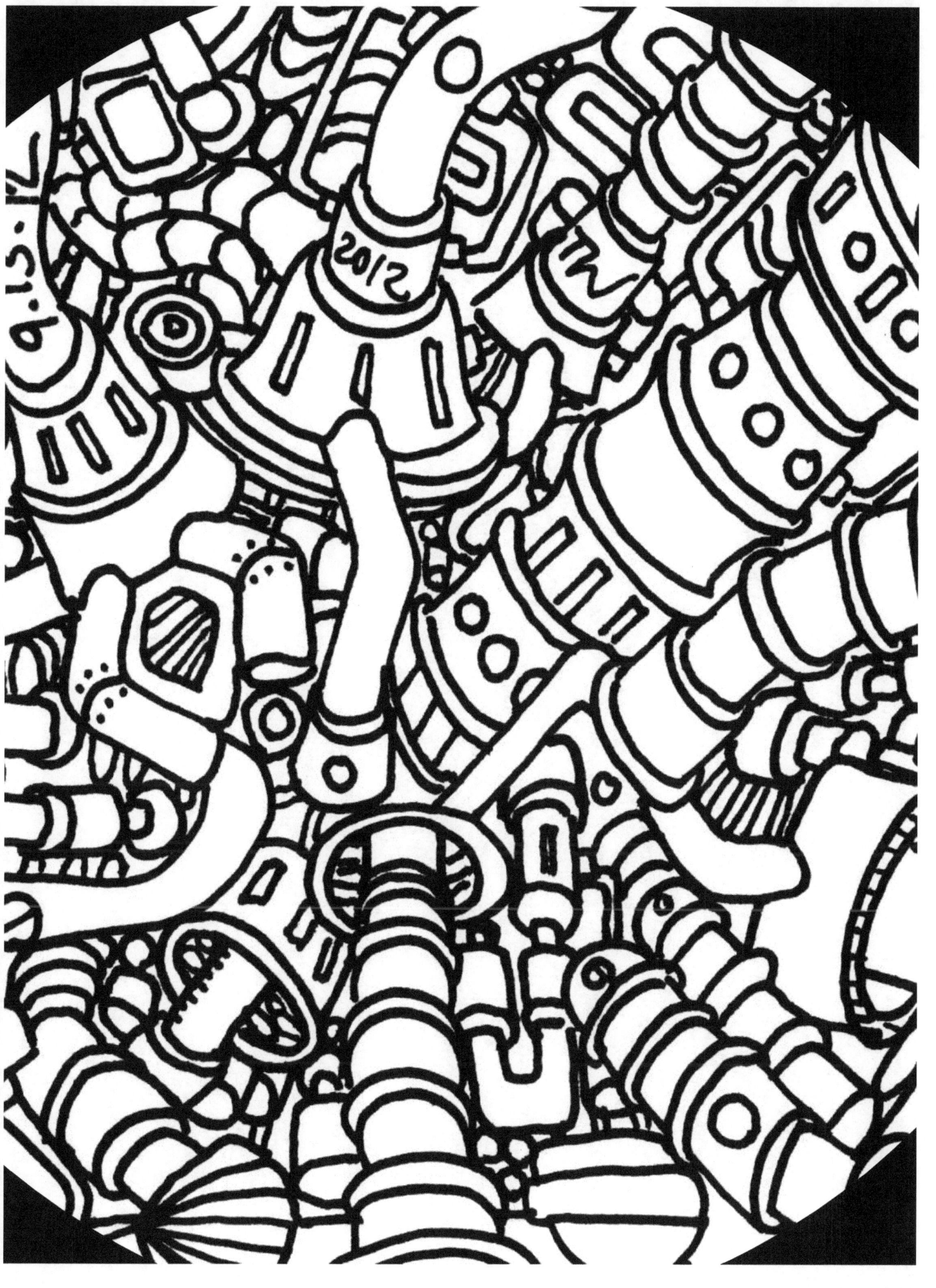

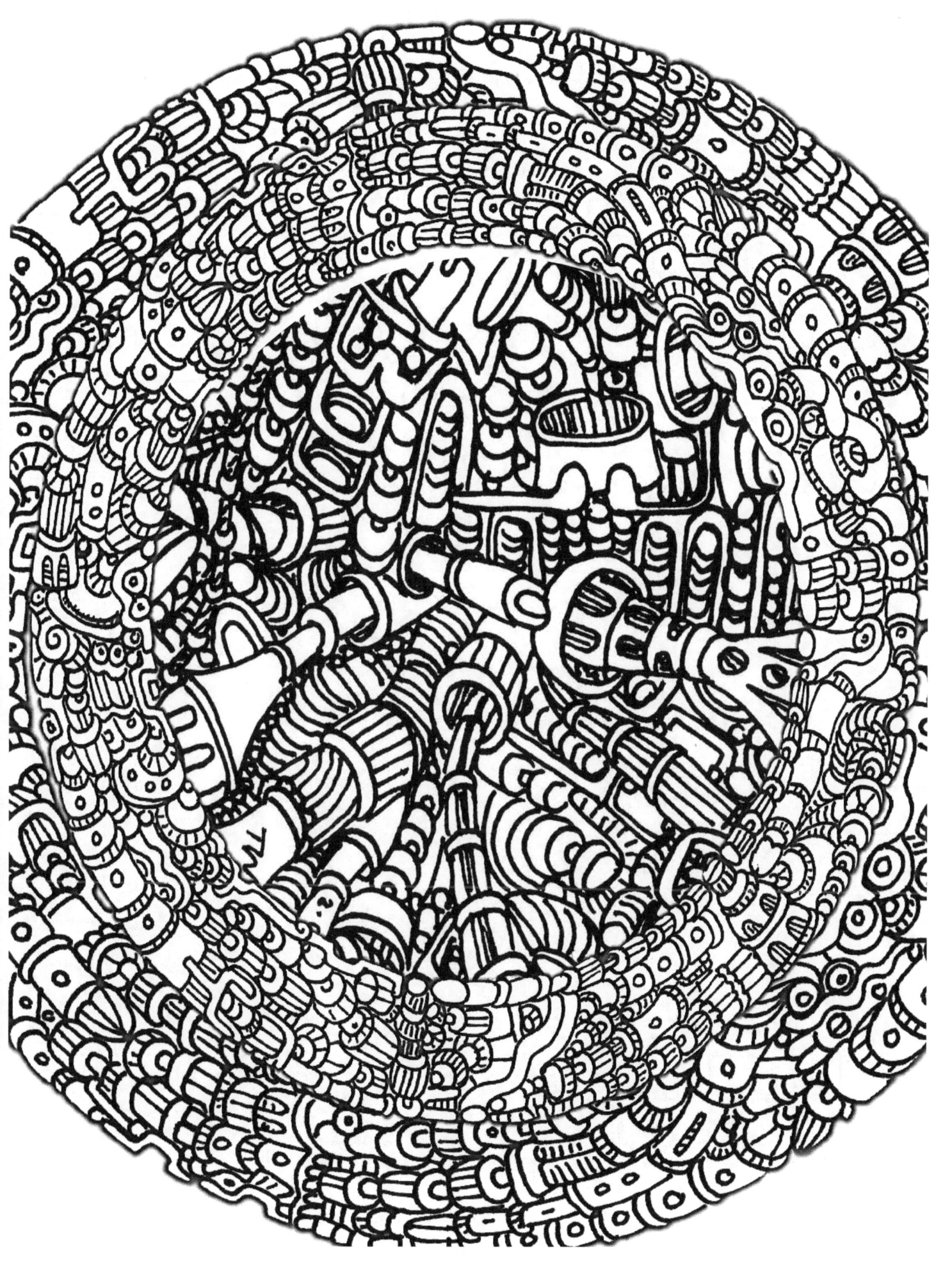

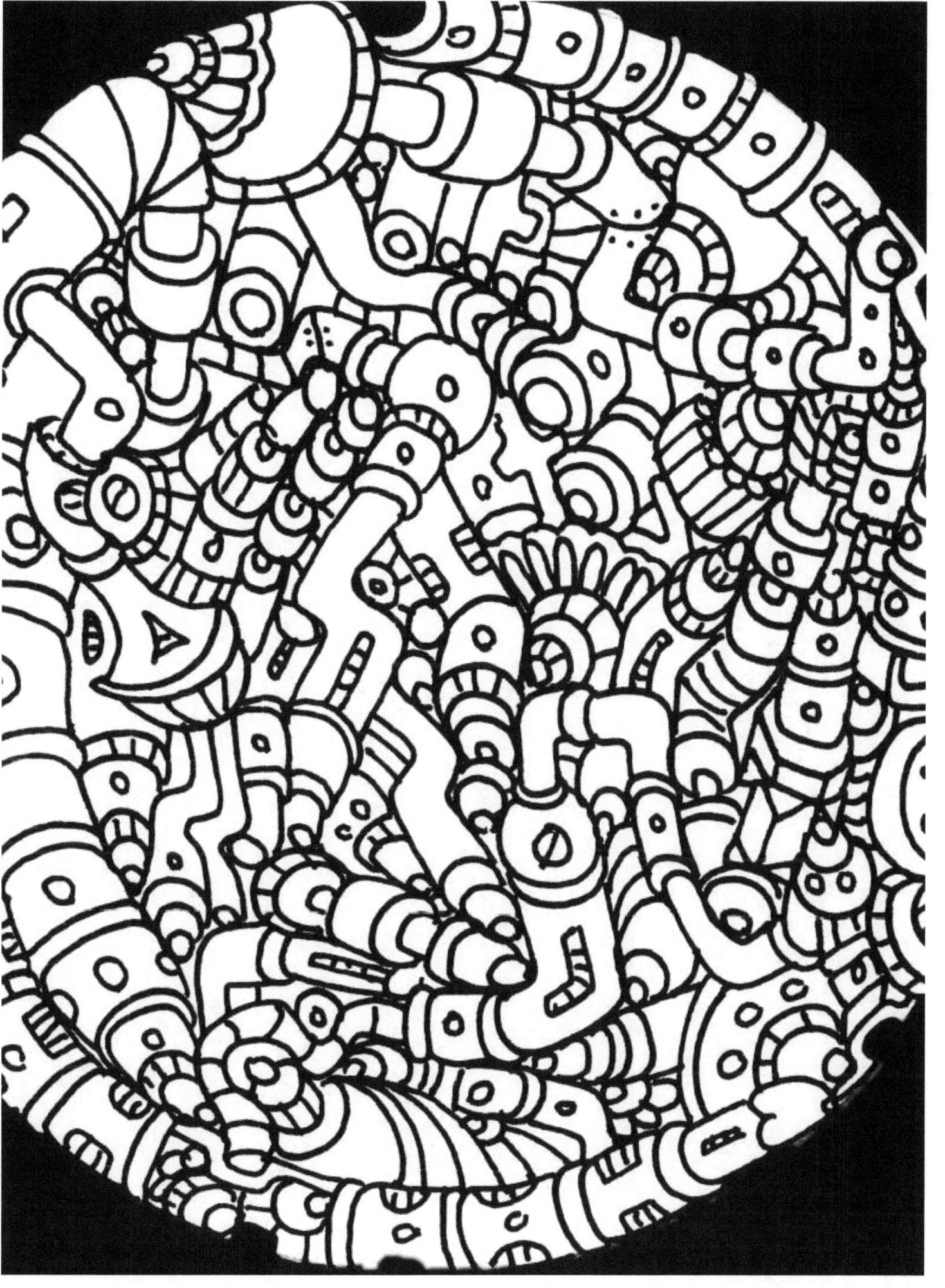

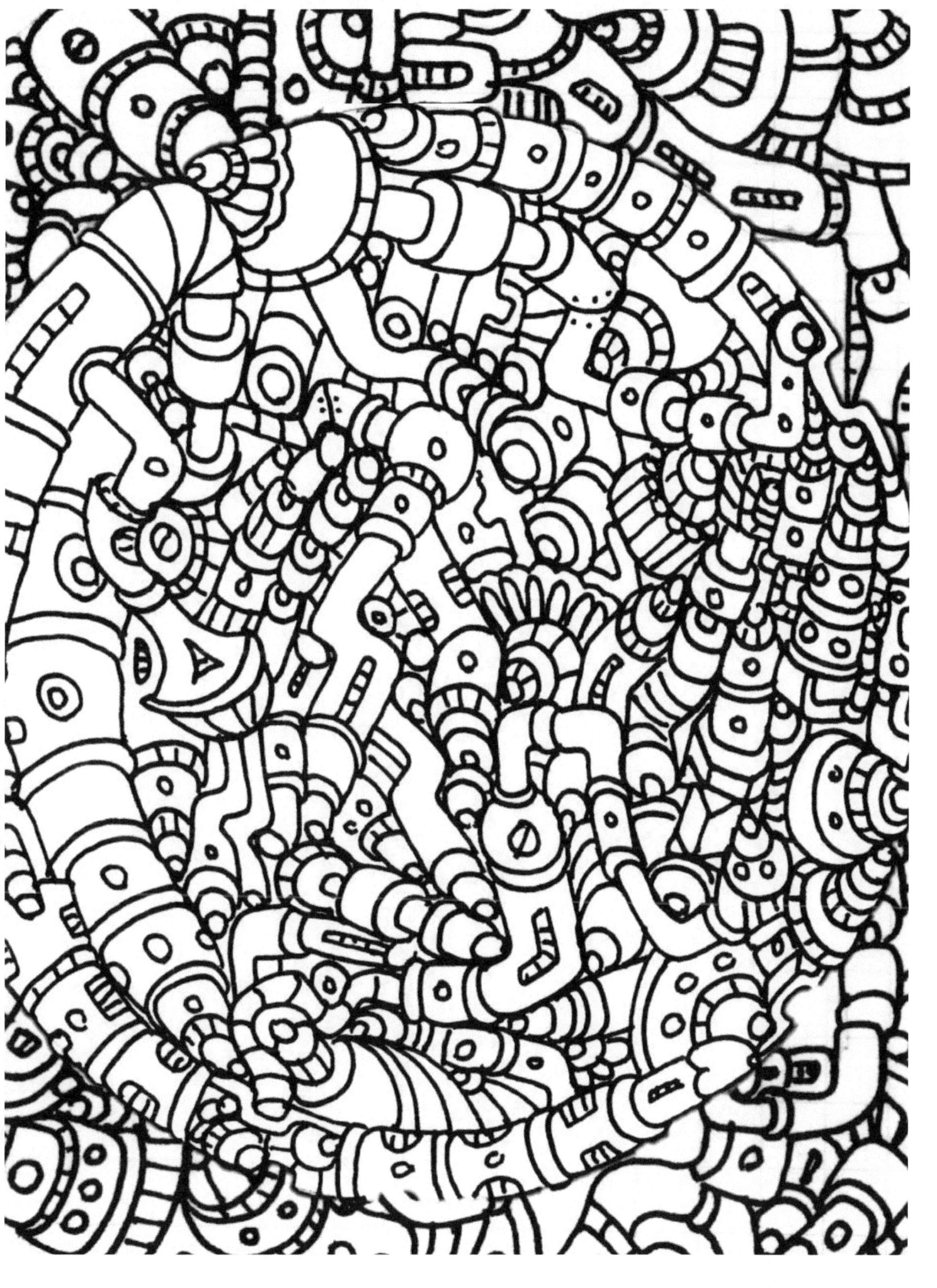

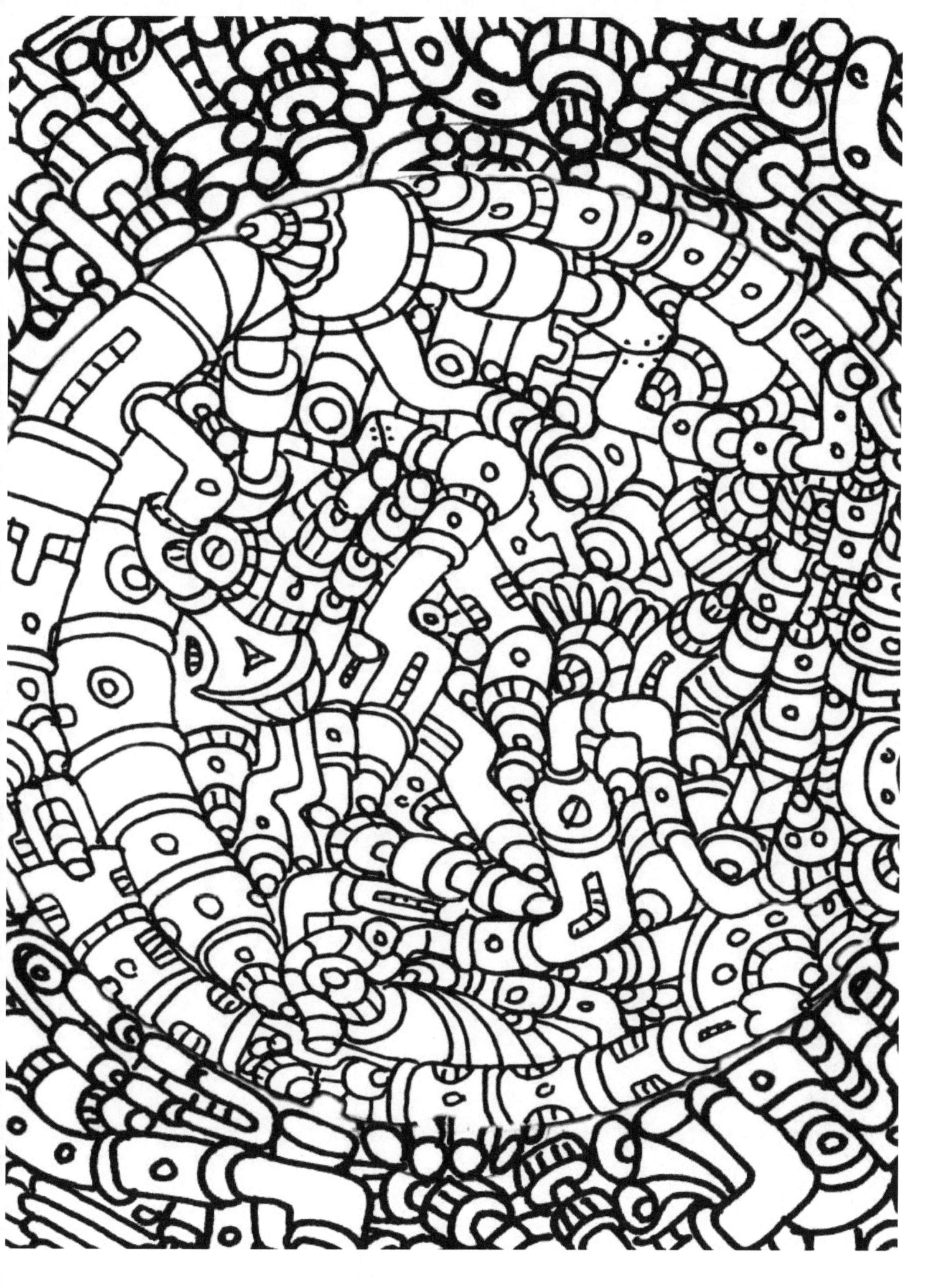

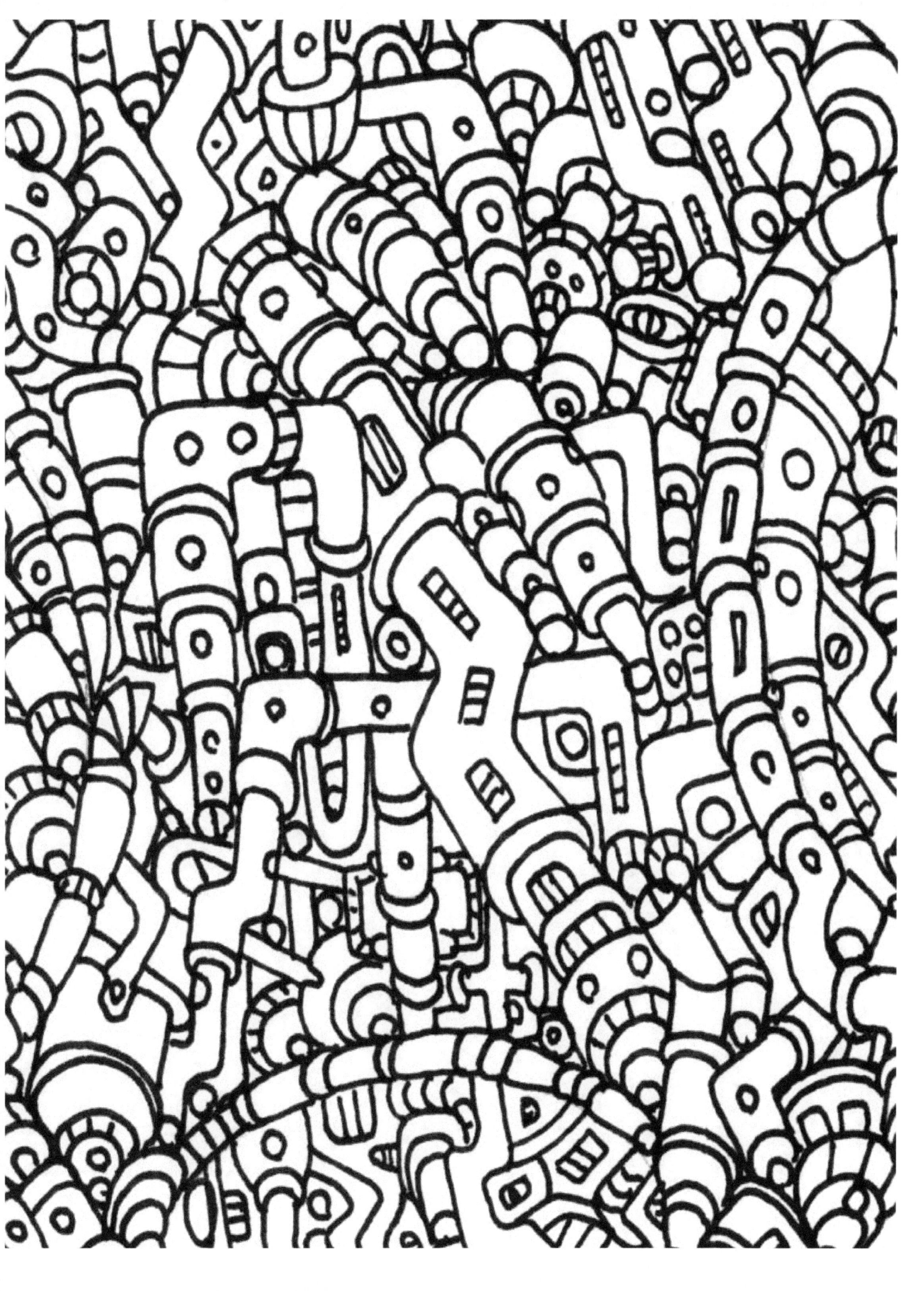

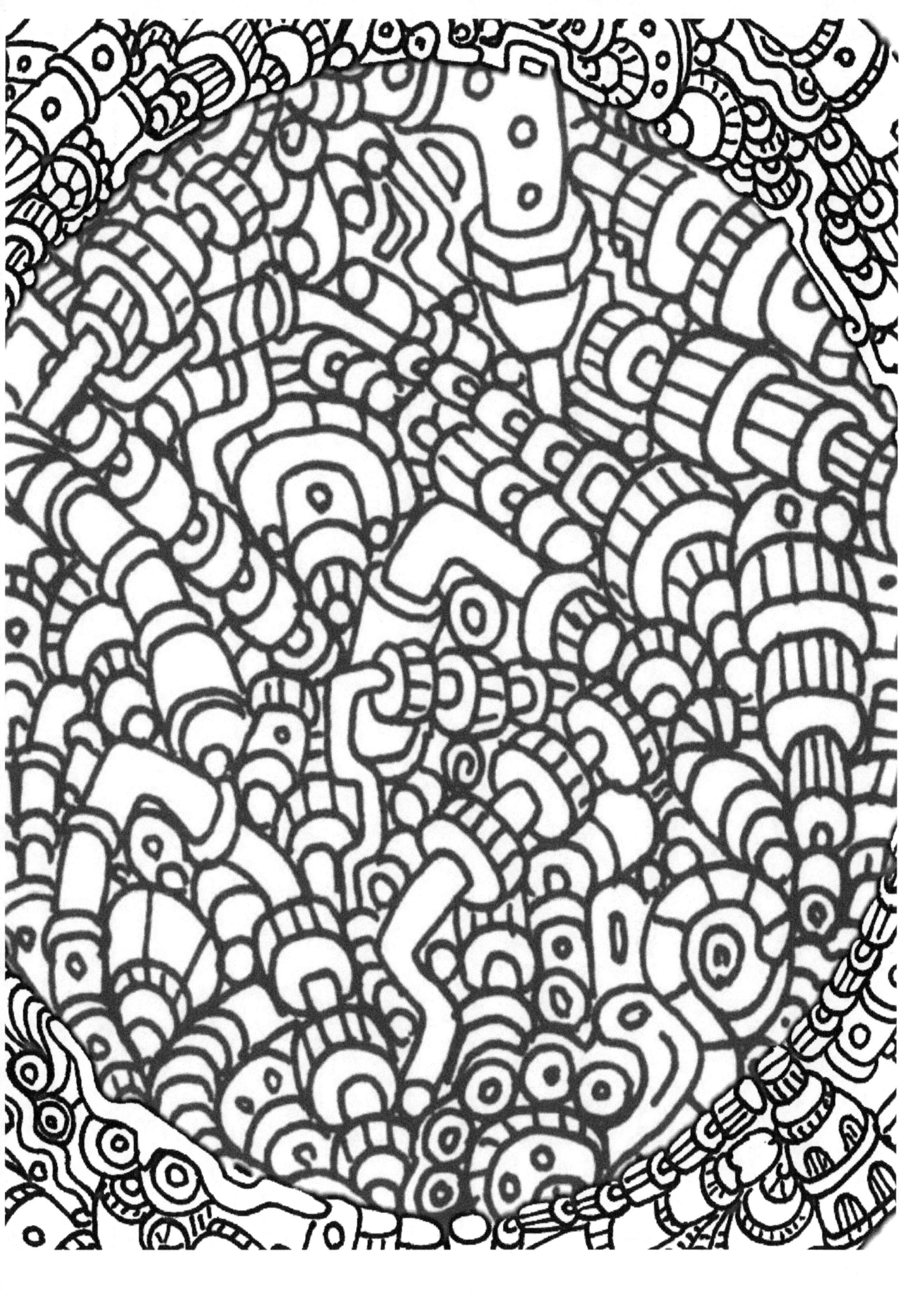

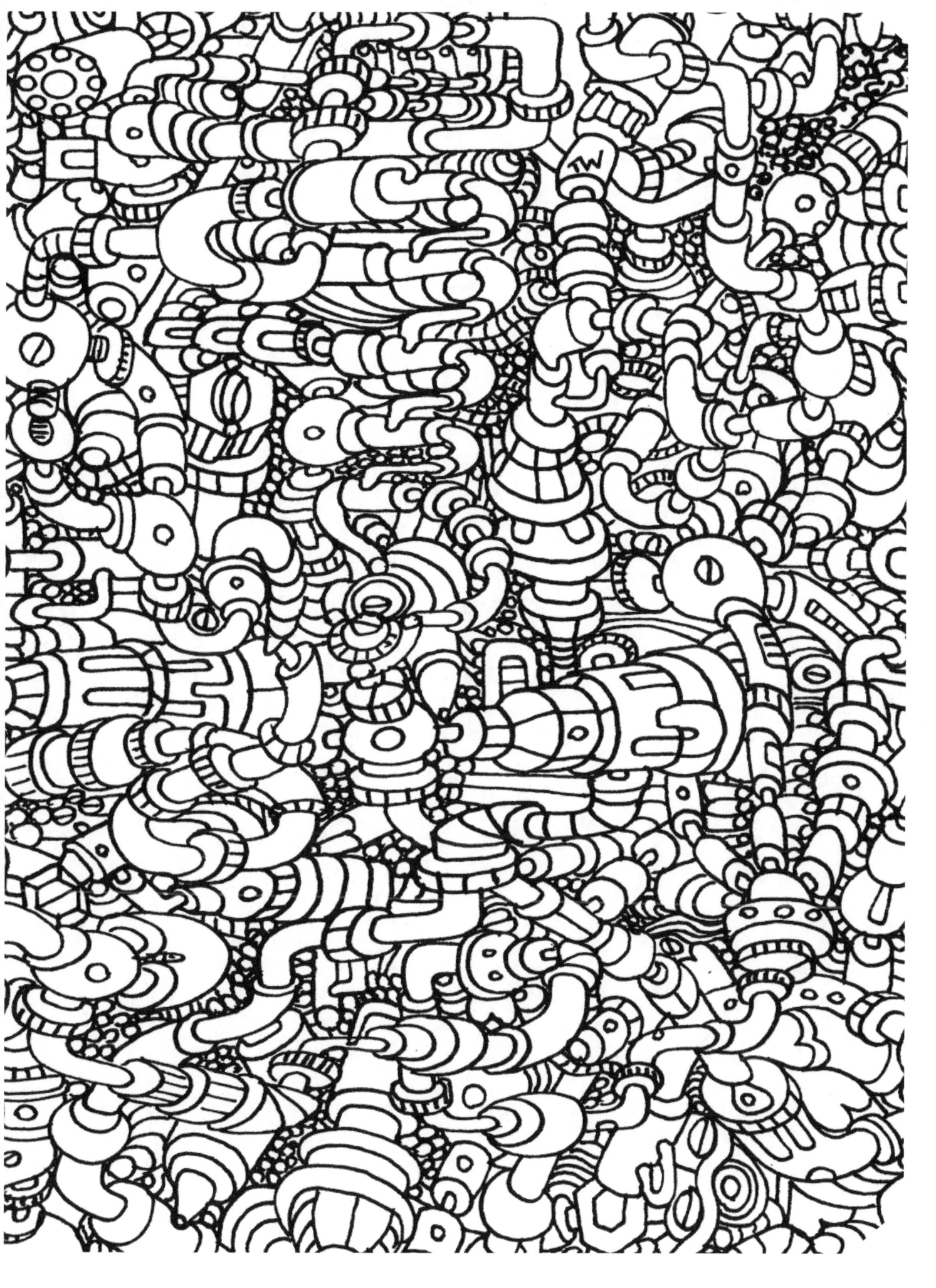

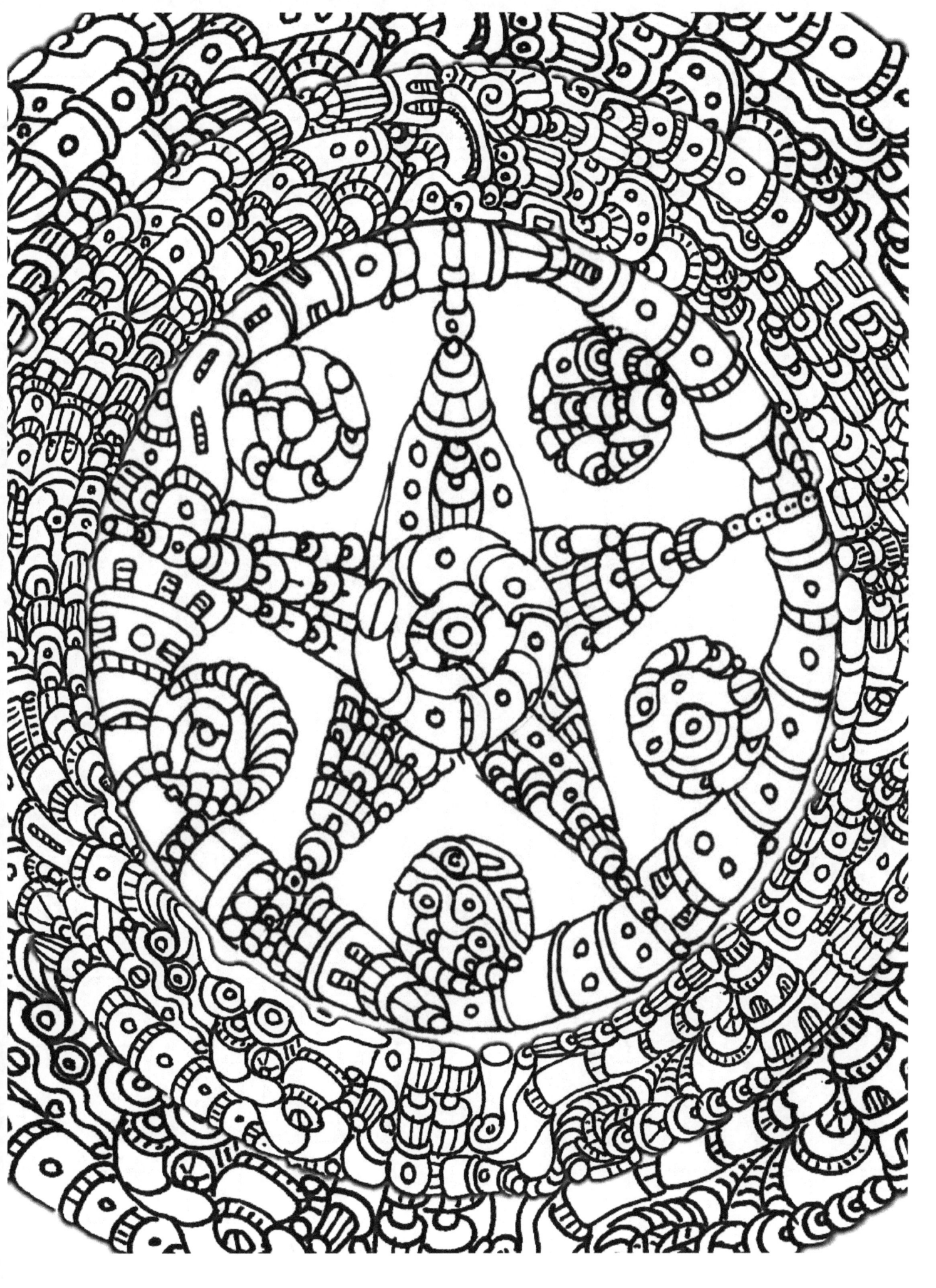

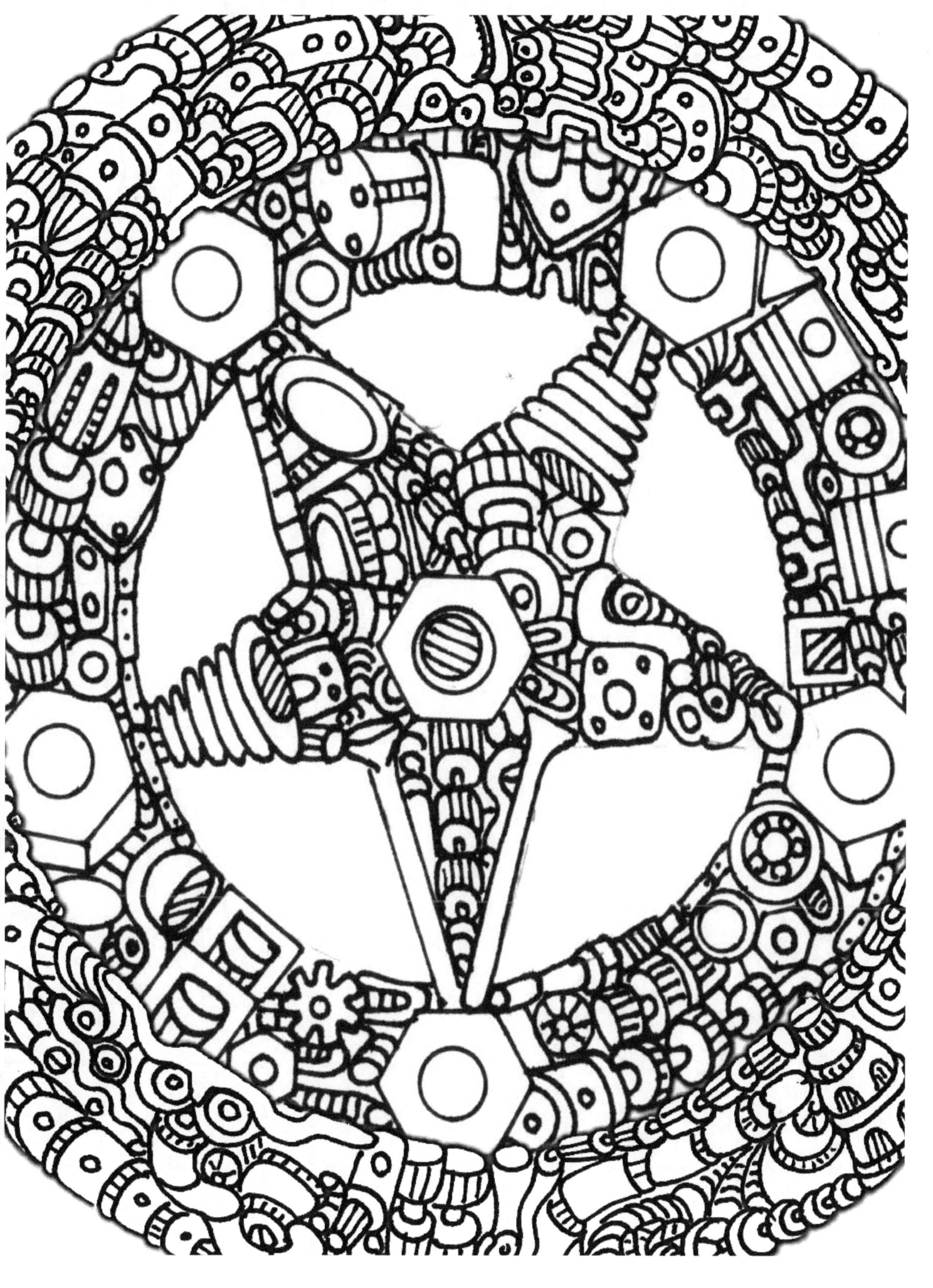

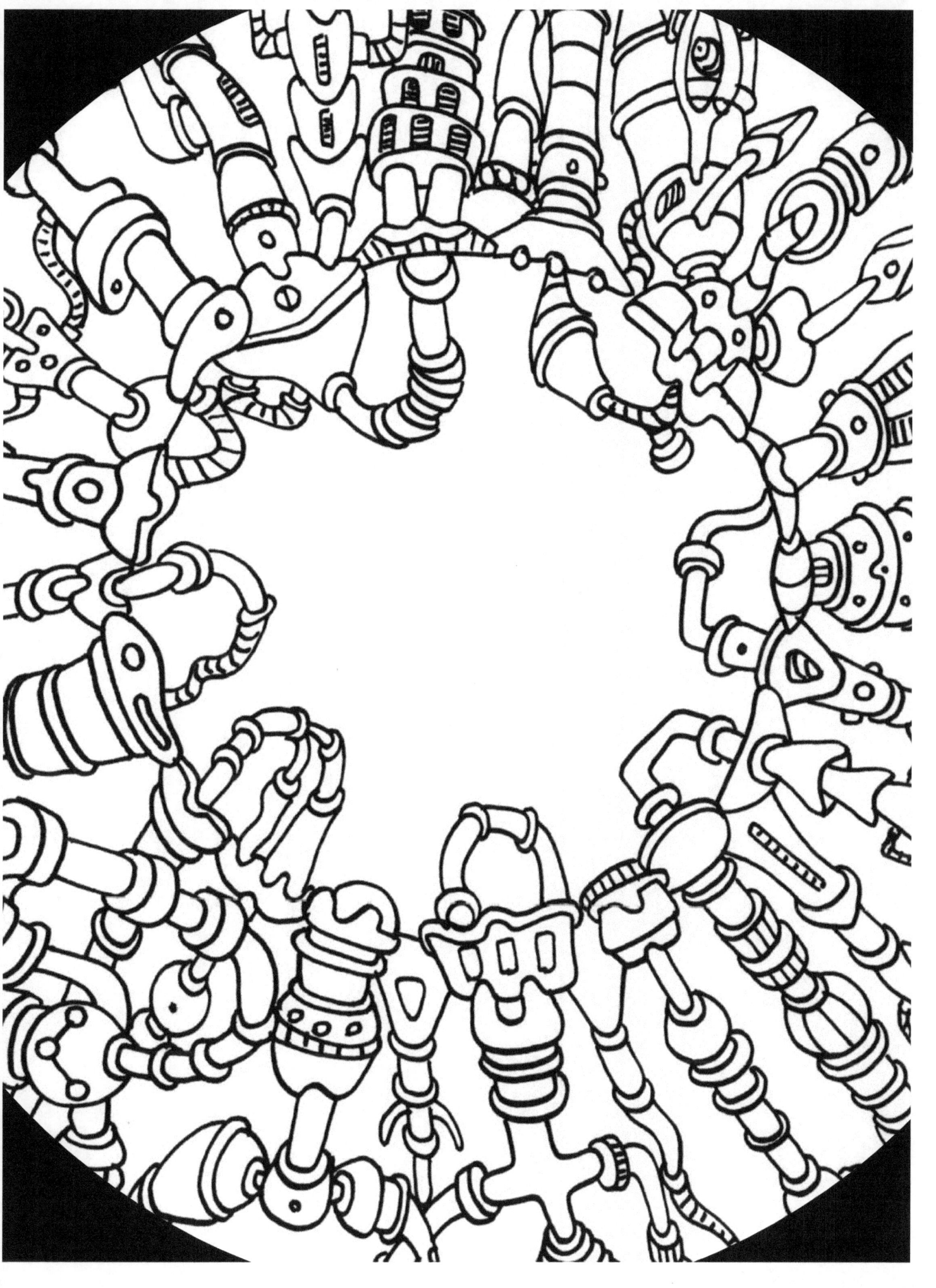

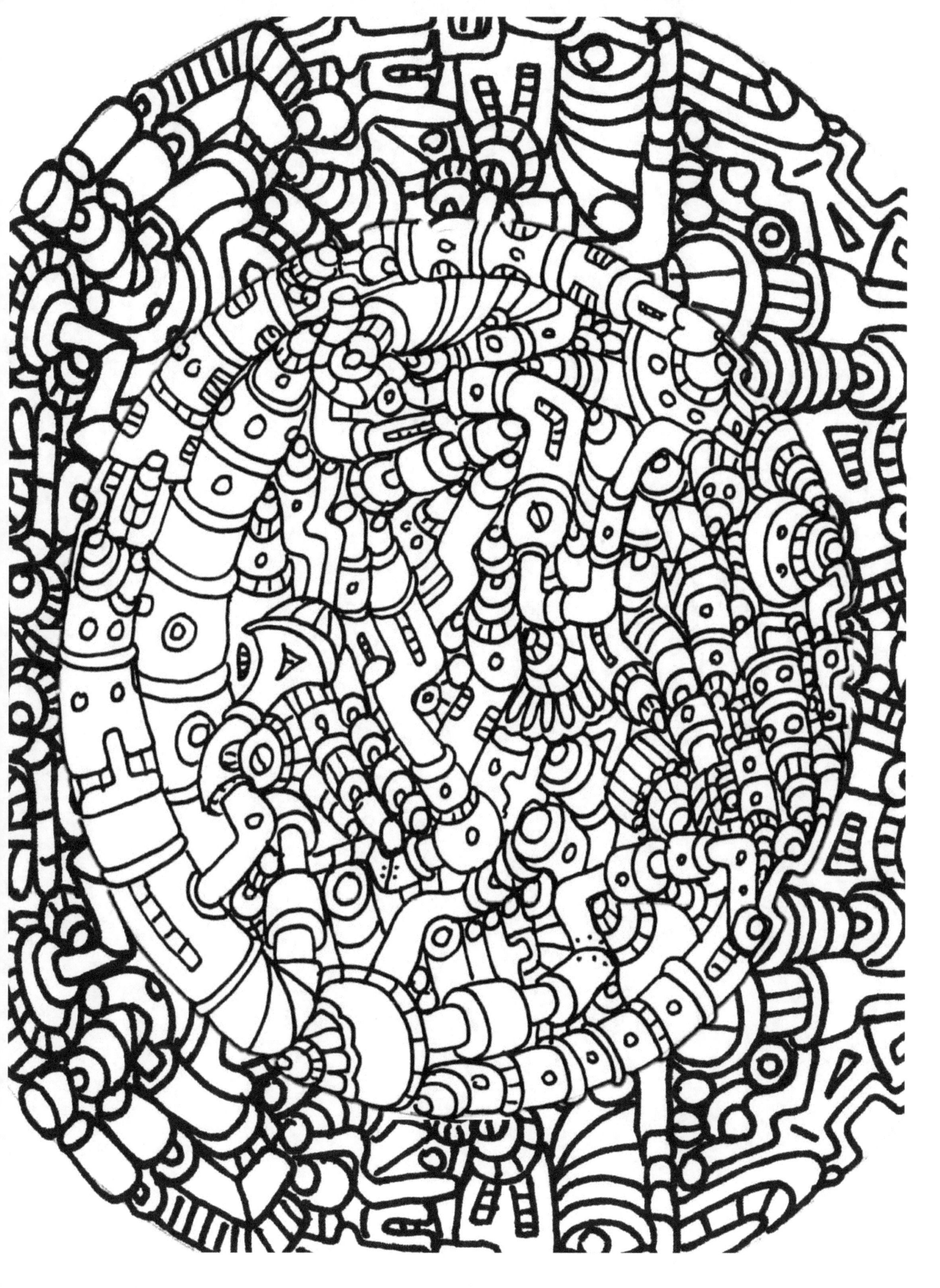

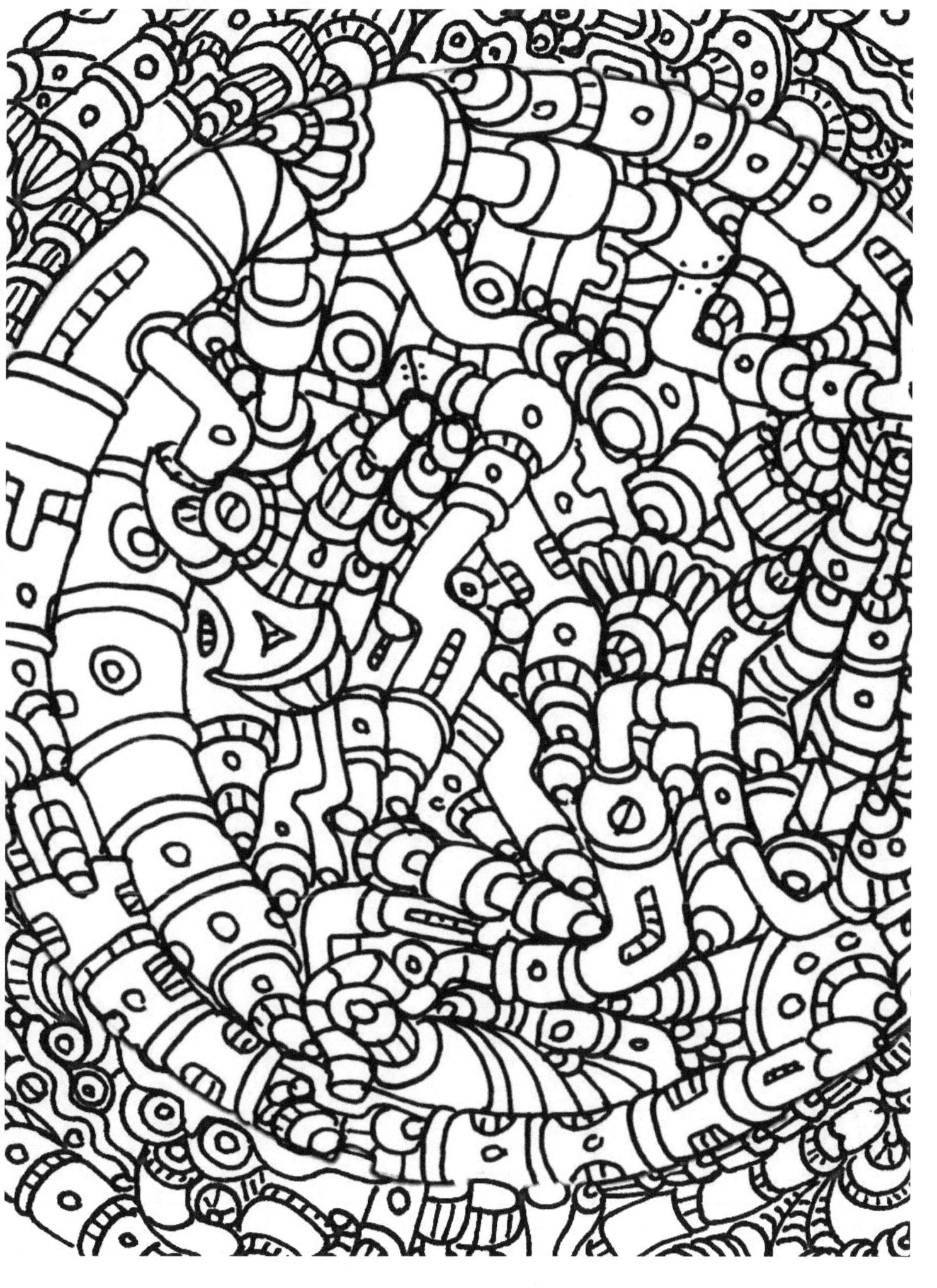

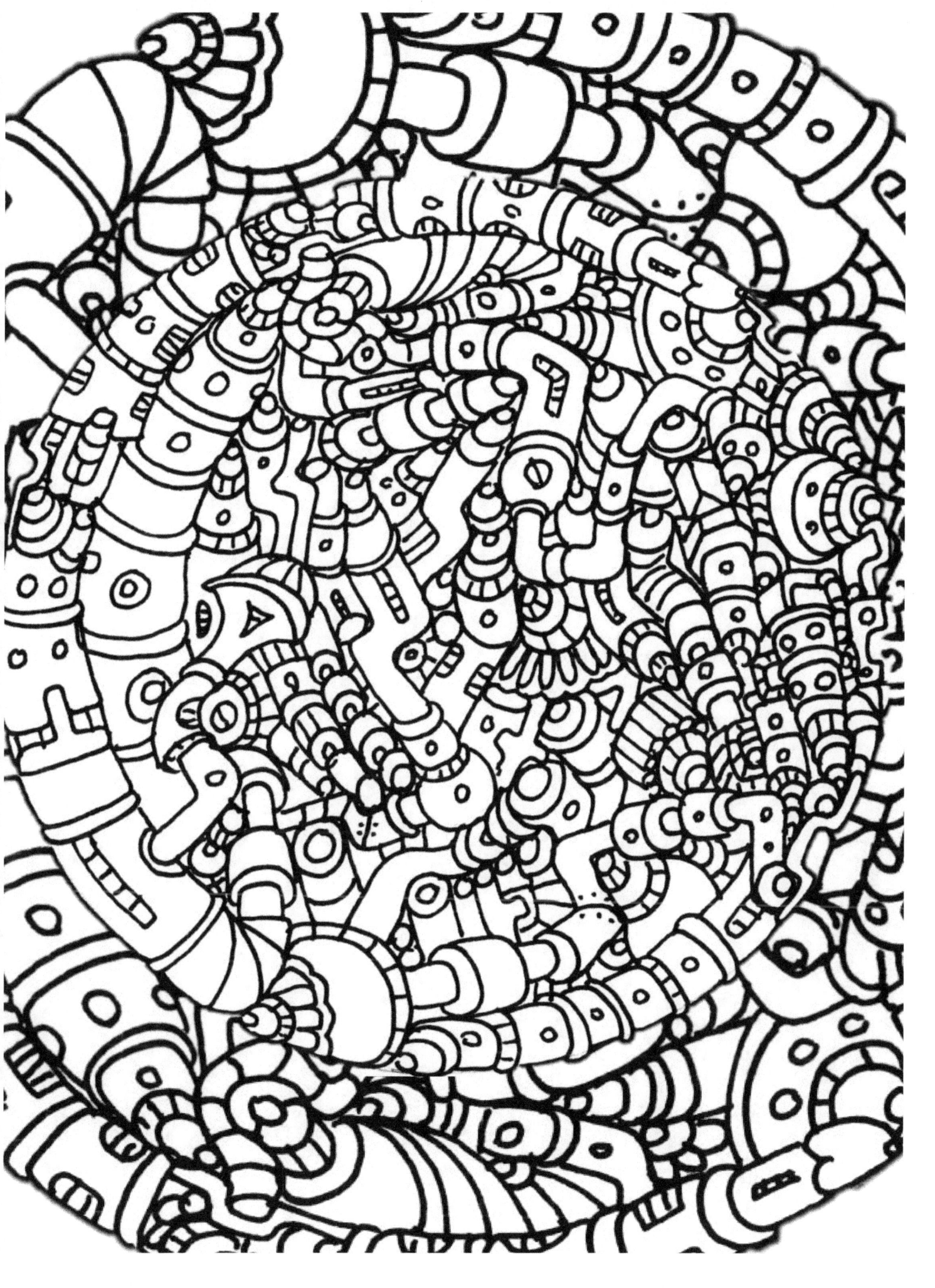

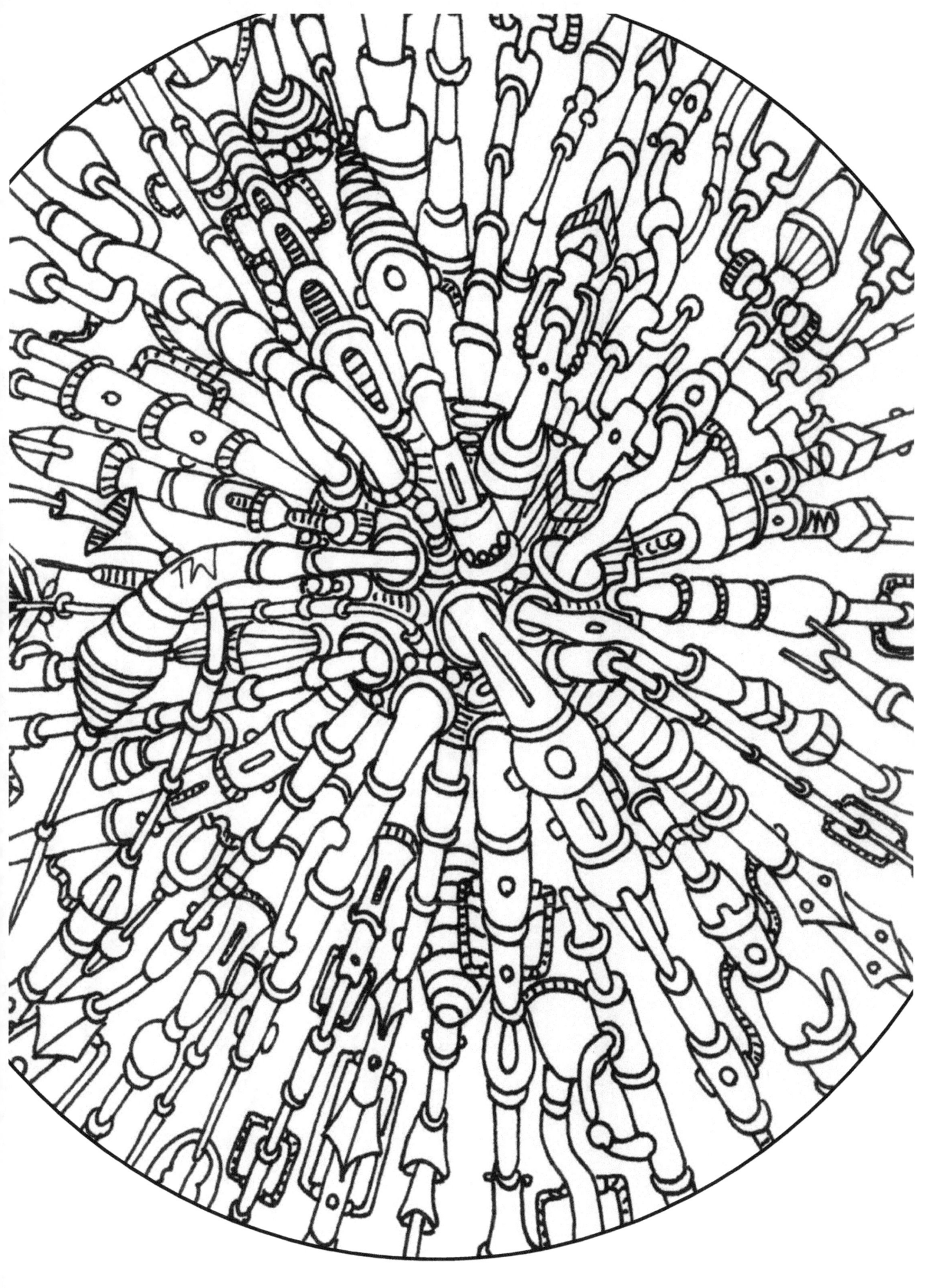

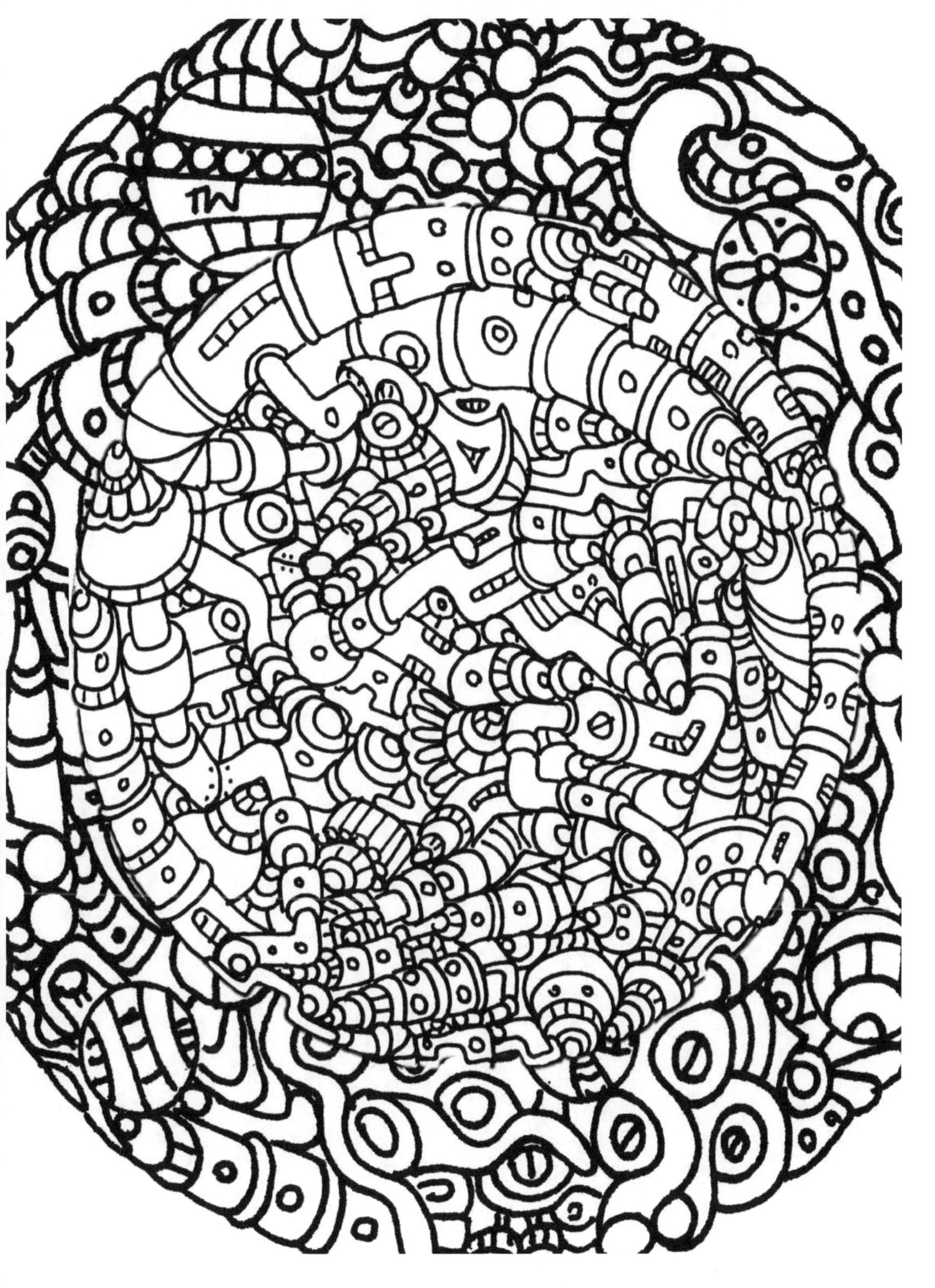

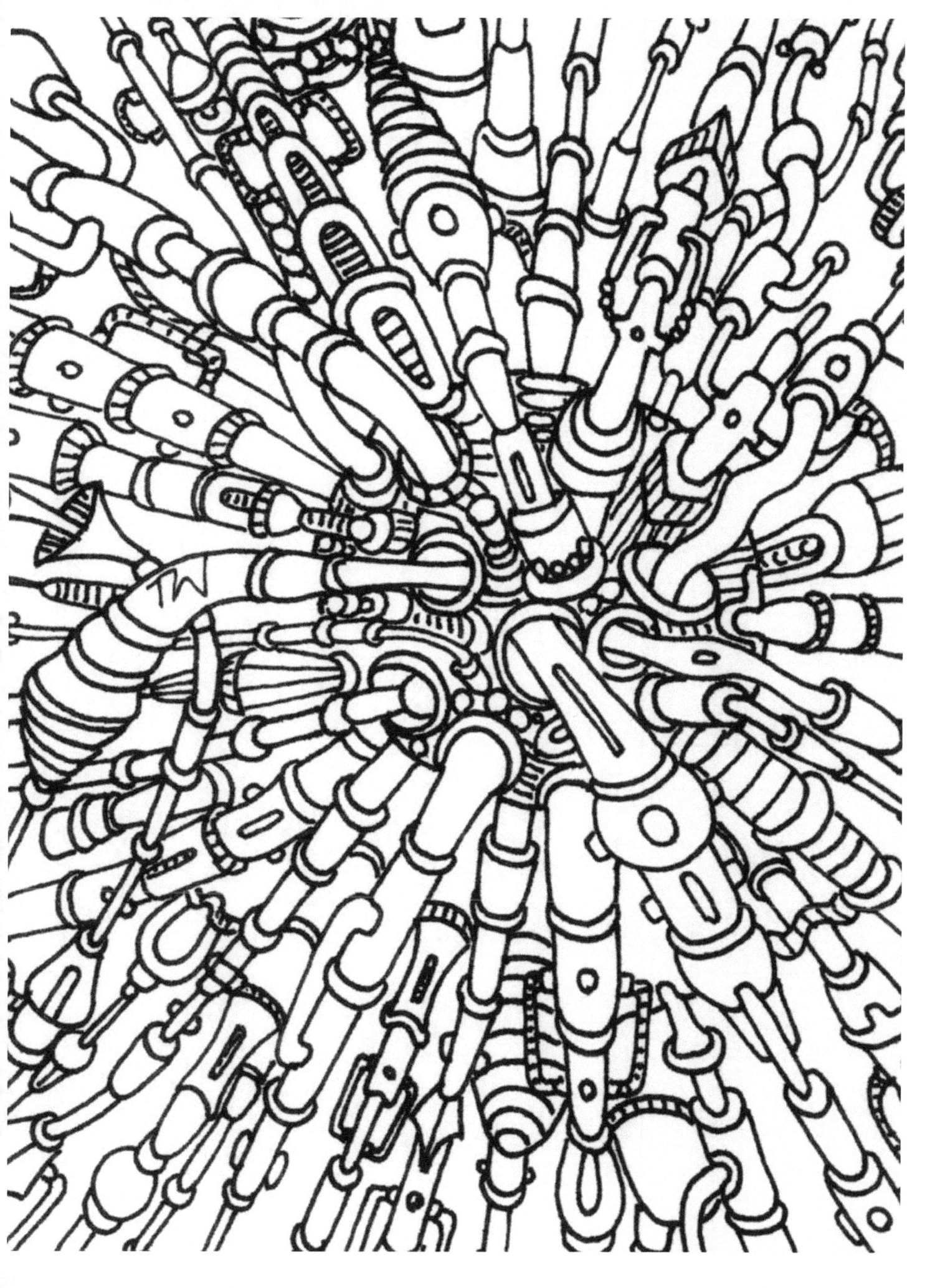

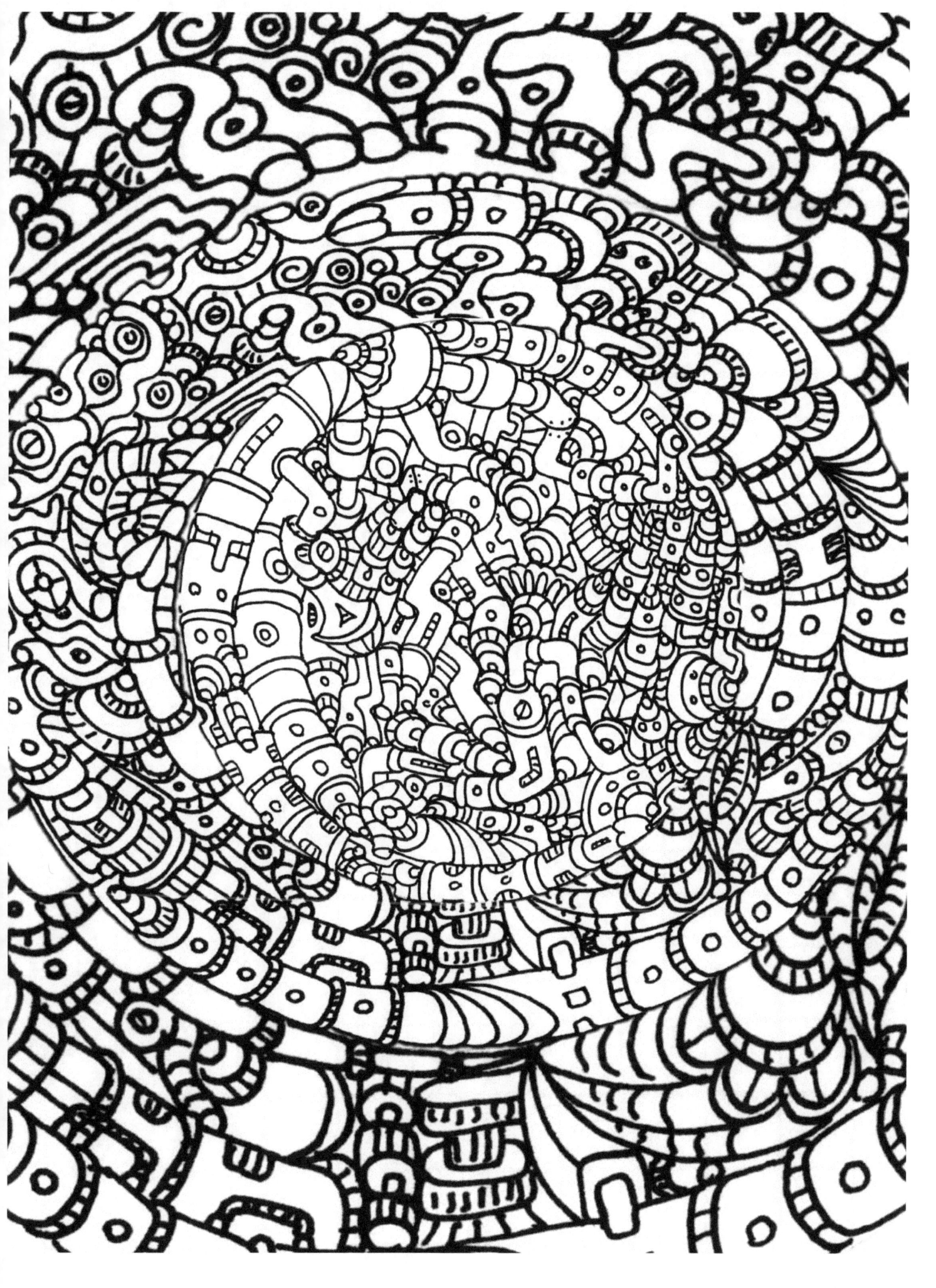

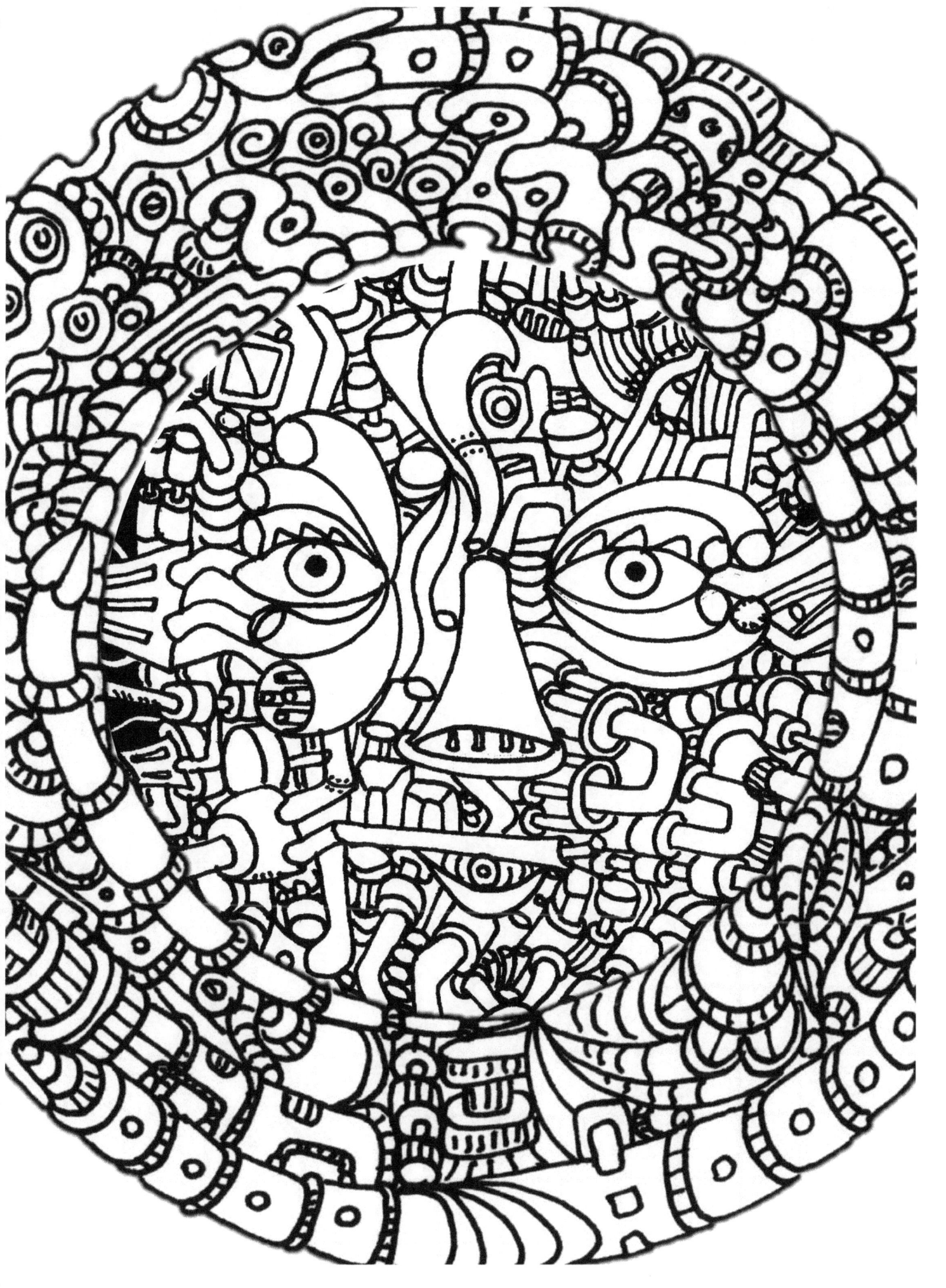

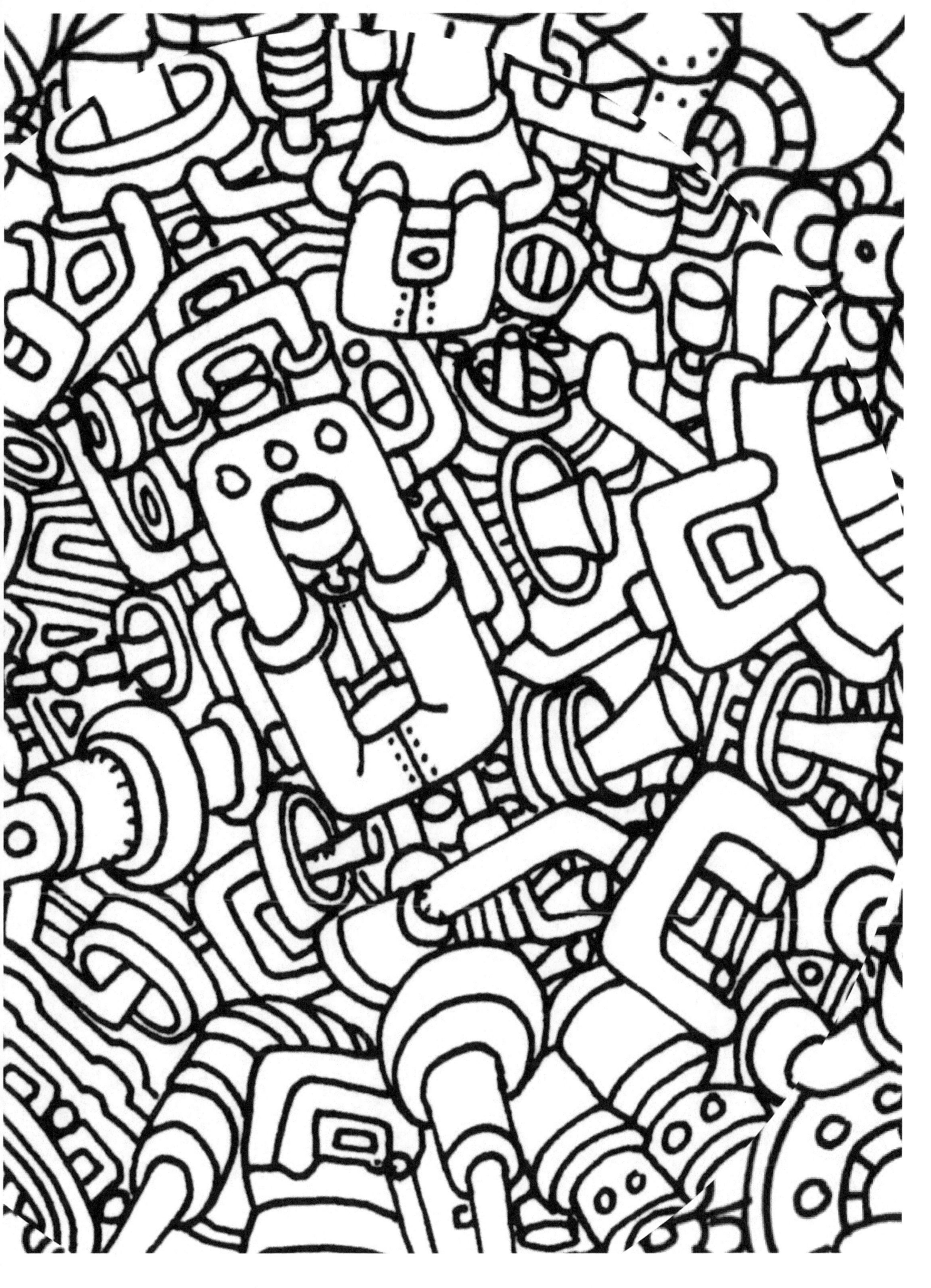

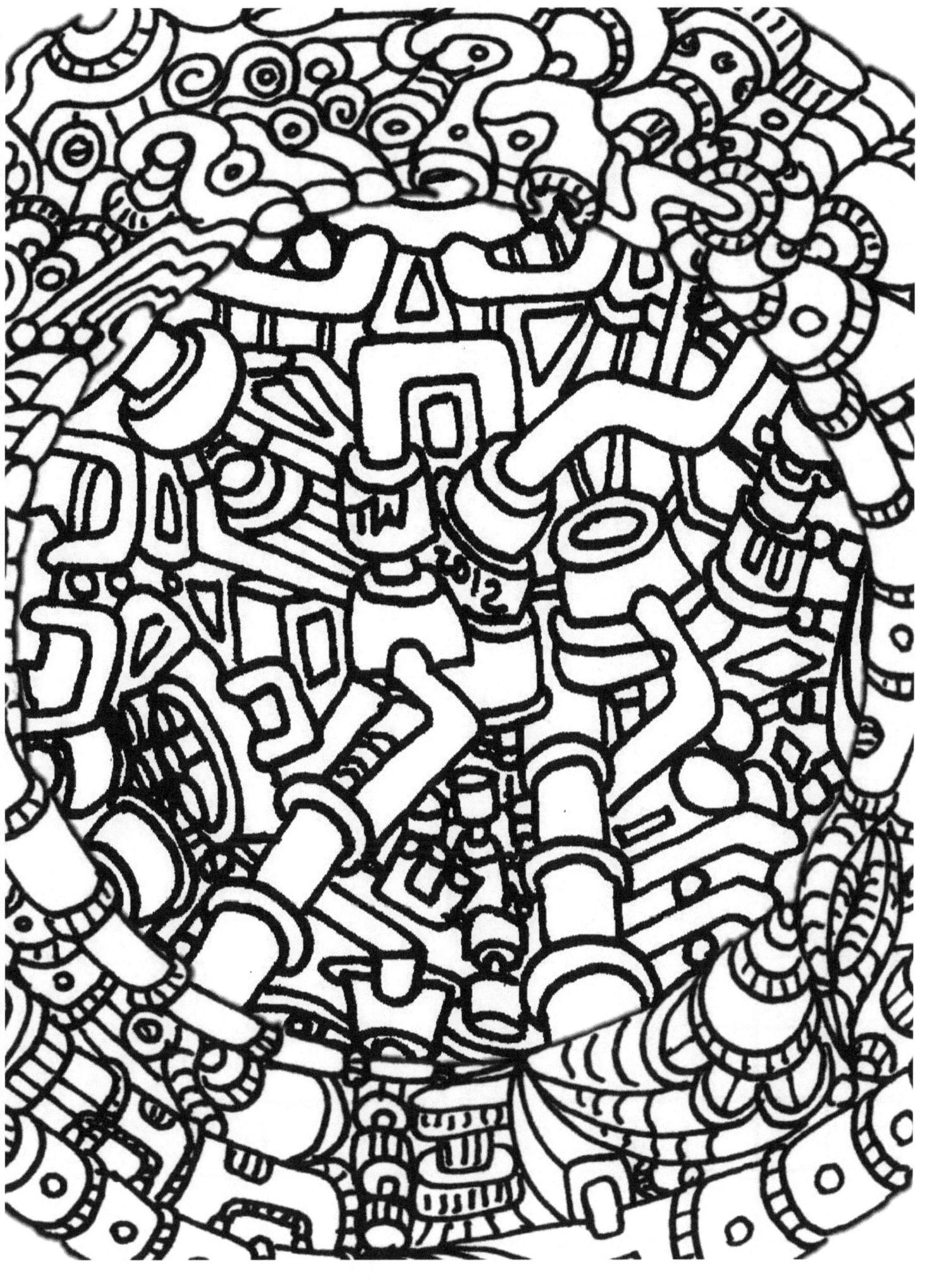

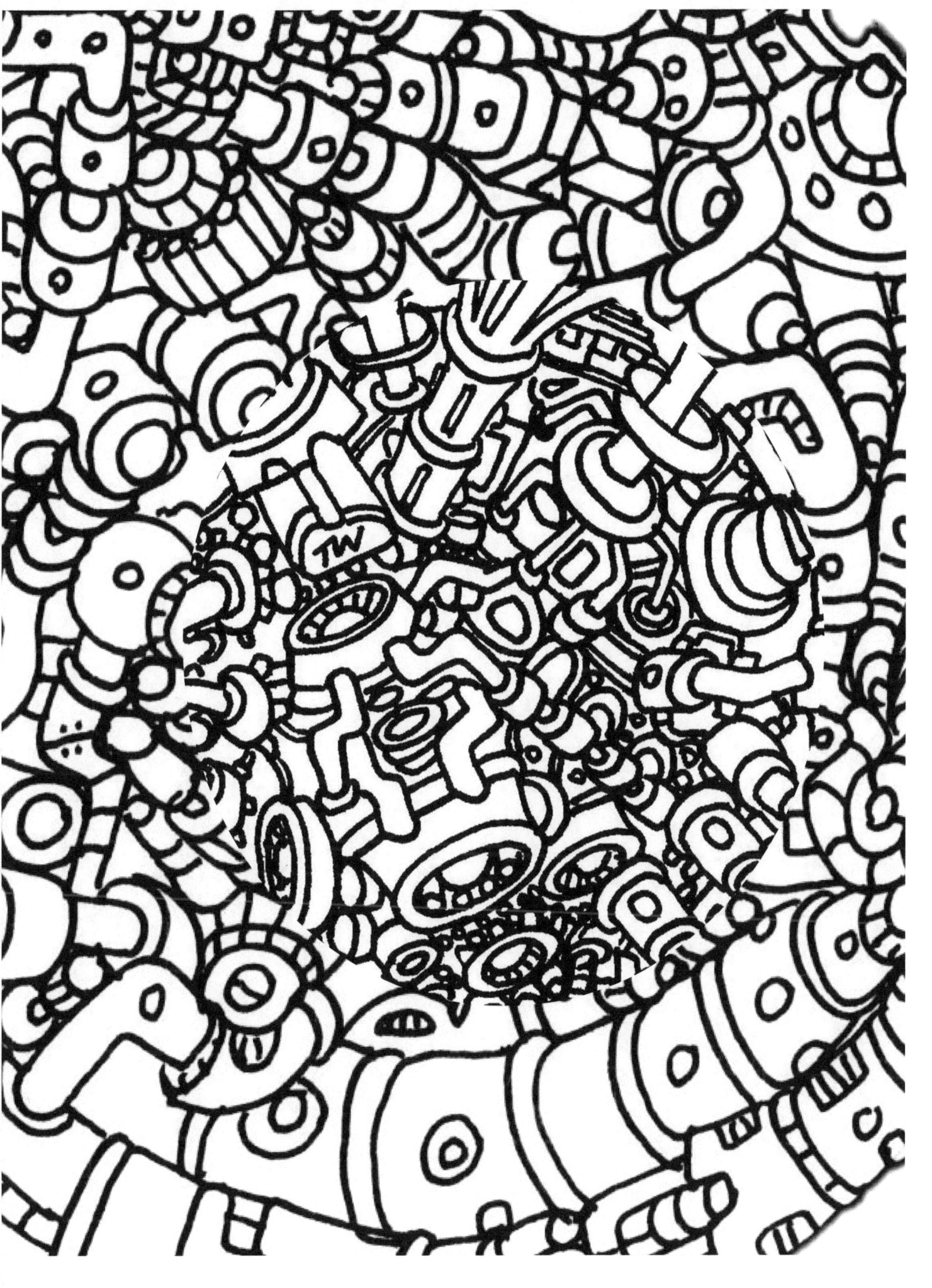